Dedication

Dedicated to my everything:

Daniel, Thomas and Oliver.

Thank you for being my amazing children xxx

Plus

A special mention for Tim – Who was always there
when my world fell apart.

The world needs more people like you.

Pages 36/37 are for you.

With Special Thanks

To Sandy and Kate Ryan

Thanks for believing in me
enough to take a chance

It was 2.36pm on a Thursday afternoon and I was happy; I mean REALLY happy. My then 2.5 year old son and I had put the Christmas tree up this morning and we'd just decorated the roof with so many decorations; it looked like our own little wonderland. It was a sunny day, and I remember the breeze playing with the curtain and the smell of freshly mowed grass was wafting through our little flat.

Just as the last box of decorations was put away I looked out the window and saw the familiar government car pull up out front; I was expecting this. An unplanned visit from DOCS – it wasn't a new thing so when they knocked on the door I let them in. I got asked the usual questions, how was I feeling? How is your mental state? Did I feel that I was coping with my 2 year old ok? Had I seen my case worker today? My answer was great, fine, yes and of course.

I remember saying it exactly like that. It's strange how I can still remember everything so distinctly; almost as if it only happened yesterday. I guess I remember it so clearly because what happened next was so UN real that I removed myself emotionally from the pain. They asked me to get a change of clothes for my little one and some pyjamas; that's weird I thought, but I did what they asked and didn't say anything.

There were two workers and when I came back into the room the lady had my little one in her arms and she stood up while the other worker gave me some papers.

I tried reading the papers but the words were blurry and I couldn't see. I asked them what they said and they told me it was an order by the court to take my baby away. The paper went into the air and I tried reaching for my baby; screaming give me back my baby GIVE ME BACK MY BABY! But the lady holding him just went towards the front door and tried to leave.

The other person kept standing in my way, so I used all my strength and pushed him out of the way. I remember seeing him fall but I didn't care! All I wanted to do was get to my baby. Only moments later the police had arrived and they were helping them take my baby away. I screamed out 'Let me say goodbye' let me give him a hug and a kiss, let me calm him down. In all the commotion he had started screaming too; so they gave him back to me and I started to calm him down, singing to him and stroking his little face. The whole time the police lady and the DOCS workers watched me.

I somehow got the opportunity to shut the front door and bolt it shut. They were outside and I was inside with my baby. I called my case worker and told her what was happening, I called my mum and told her what was going on. This couldn't be happening, it was all so surreal … I saw it all unwinding in front of me but I was numb to it all.

The only thing I was sure of was that no matter what I was going to keep my baby!

The police were pounding on the door, open the door or we will break it down. We have a court order they were saying. I went around the flat and shut all the windows so that they couldn't get in through there. I turned the music up loud so that the shouting didn't upset my baby and we just sat in the middle of the floor holding onto each other.

After a few minutes I heard my case managers voice break through the music; she was asking me to let her in; but I couldn't trust anyone anymore so I ignored her and turned the music up some more. This was the end of everything good in my life; from this point on my life just went downhill.

I remember hearing glass breaking and hands all over me, rough hands that were prying my arms away from around my baby and holding me back as they took him away. He was crying out 'mummy, mummy, mummy, mummy over and over. I was screaming out 'give me back my baby, give me back my baby' but it was useless. They strapped him into the car seat and drove him away. After they let me stand up I pulled a knife from out of my top and I just put it to my throat. I can't remember when I put the knife there, but it was in my hands and I wasn't going to let it go!

The police went from holding me down like a criminal to pulling their guns on me. Yelling at me to lower my weapon. But I didn't care anymore.

I told them to just shoot me so I didn't have to feel the pain anymore. I begged them to take their guns and shoot me right in the heart so that it would stop beating and stop all the hurt.

The police lady stepped forward and through my crying I heard her say 'Hannah please don't make me shoot you, I only just graduated from the academy last week. Please don't make me use my gun on you; you're not the bad guy' I was listening to her speak and didn't see the other officer sneak up behind me.

When I was knocked to the ground I didn't fight them anymore. I just let them handcuff me and put me in the back of the police car.

It was only as they were driving me away that I looked up and saw that everyone was outside, everyone that had heard the screaming had come outside to see. My neighbours above me were telling the police that they were dogs for taking my baby away, told them they should be out catching the real criminals. The man next door was just shaking his head in disbelief and the lady over the road said 'I will fix the window love and keep an eye on your place while you're gone'.

After a few minutes the lady officer started talking to me, saying I will put in a good word for you. I will tell my sergeant that your place looked so full of love and that your baby was holding on to you so tight. I will tell him that you weren't going to hurt anyone and that you only pulled the knife after your baby was taken away. I will tell him all of that Hannah.

She reached over the seat and took the handcuffs off; and as she leaned over she whispered in my ear 'I'm so sorry they took your baby away'.

Rather than take me to the station they took me to the emergency department for a psych assessment.

Because I had to go to court the next day for DOCS they agreed to send me back home after 4 hours; I wasn't a threat to anyone they said and I had only been reacting to the situation. Most of what they said was true, the only thing that wasn't was the part about me not being a threat to anyone. I was a threat to myself.

So I was sent home and when I got out of the taxi my neighbours started coming out of their front doors to see me.

Rather than see me as a problem neighbour; they saw me for all my pain. They made me food and bought me cups of tea; they told me that the police came back after they dropped me off and said that they weren't going to press charges. They were going to back me up in court if I needed them too. I didn't hear most of what they said because all I wanted to do was go to bed and never wake up. Having my baby taken away by strangers was having my reason for existence taken away.

When the last person left at 11.27pm, I went and stood under the shower; then when the crying became too much, I sat in the shower hugging my legs and rocked back and forth until the water ran cold.

It was 12.34am when I got into bed. I thought about taking a handful of pills but I had to be in court at 9am; so I just laid motionless on the bed not moving, not feeling, not believing that the day before was even real; until I finally fell asleep.

My alarm went off at 7.35am and like a robot I got ready to go to court. It was raining that day, but I didn't care. I just walked to the train station, got a train and showed up at the children's court.

For hours I sat waiting for my case to be called, I had no one to talk to, no one there to support me, no one to ask me was I okay. It was just me against the world.

At 3.20pm they called my name over the speaker and told me to go to court 4. When I got there the lawyer sent to represent me did all the talking, I just sat there motionless to it all. Barely paid attention to what was being said until the magistrate asked me why had I pulled a knife in the presence of my child?

I argued that he had been driven away; but because it was what the DOCS workers had put in their paperwork, he said 'I tend to believe what they have said' So I reacted and told him that yes; I had wanted to slit my throat and make them watch so they could see what they had done. I blamed them for taking away not only my son, but my reason to live. My EVERYTHING that meant anything to me was taken away and given to strangers to look after because according to 'the experts' they could look after him better than me!

I know looking back that this wasn't helpful and that when it comes to DOCS and them taking a child away, they will fabricate the evidence they need to support their actions and no matter the real truth they will always win in the end.

I left court at 5.35pm with a notice to appeal a decision, with a court date in the future about 6 weeks away. This was the worst possible outcome.

I got the train home and again walked in the rain back home. I wouldn't answer the door when the neighbours knocked and I didn't change out of my clothes that were soaked through. I just fell against the door as it closed and shutdown mentally and physically.

When I got up from the floor I went to the medicine cabinet and took the last 30 Valium that I had left. Put on some music, laid on the couch and waited for the darkness to cover me. I didn't give a fuck about what happened anymore. My reason to go on was gone and I couldn't get him back. Everyone who I thought I could trust had either turned on me or taken the side of DOCS. When the Valium started taking effect I didn't fight it or even get scared because as far as I was concerned, I had nothing left to live for.

Three days later I was in hospital with carbon monoxide poisoning. When I woke up from the Valium hangover I felt like shit; even more so when I realized that I had no more Valium left. I was intent on ending my life so I backed my car into the garage, blocked up the tailpipe and fed the hose through the window.

Then I put the car in idle; put on a cd and cried until I started to feel sleepy. At the time I had no idea how to do what I was doing, whether it was going to work or even if I had enough petrol to make it work.

One of my support workers came to the house and couldn't find me, he came to the garage and heard the car. He was banging on the door, begging me to get out of the car; but I couldn't move or answer. I heard him on the phone with the emergency services telling them that he was scared that it was too late.

A few minutes later I hear the wail of an ambulance and the police then the sound of the garage door being kicked in and broken down. The police smashed the side window to get the doors unlocked and the paramedics got me out.

I was really sick. I had pneumonia PLUS carbon monoxide poisoning, and I didn't care. The longer I fought the doctors, the more risk at risk I was of getting brain damage. Even though I knew this, I still tried to run away from the doctors and I lashed out any way I could. In the end they had to get me a special nurse, to watch my every move.

For three weeks I stayed in hospital, first on the wards then in the psychiatric unit. But finally I got to see my baby again! It was supervised but at least I got to hug him and hold him tight. It always hurt to let him go, but in the end it happened so often that we got used to it.

The goodbyes became less often as I started to get him more. We moved into a nice new place and things finally started to look up.

After 11 months I finally got my baby back! I still had a long way to go, many more court dates. Many more hurdles to jump over, that at times left me hurt and bruised; but each and every time I got stronger.

This was that beginning of a fight that took a good part of 5 years of my life and precious time off my baby boy that I will never get back.

Countless court hearings, so many in fact that I stopped counting when it got to 45.

I had 58 hospital admissions for mental health issues; with overdoses and self -harm at the top of the list.

3 different addresses.

And today; nearly 8 years since that day when they took my baby away, I still cry when I think about the cruel way in which they handled the whole thing. DOCS had not gathered the relevant information, and instead of calling all my supports to find out if my mental state was stable, they acted on old facts.

Had they made those calls, they would have been told that my mental state had improved and that I had had a longer more stable period of wellness than I had in a long time.

As a result of their actions; my children could have been without a mother. They took away my reason to live and expected me to be okay.

When I told them this, they told me I needed to find another reason to get out of bed every day. ARE YOU FUCKING SERIOUS?!

Who or what the fuck else could I possibly find to 'replace' the needs and wants of a child of 2 years old? What better reason in life is there to get up out of bed every day other than your child?! Nothing. Not a damn thing; but they didn't get it. Never understood that my entire reason for still being alive was to be a mother to my child that they took away.

Tell me this, if someone took your child away and told a court that strangers could do a better job than you, wouldn't you want to die to? I love my children and it is only by sheer courage and determination that I am still here to be a mother to them.

DOCS were wrong in this case and now it is me against them to get help with trying to rectify the damage.

They are the ones that have to make the other services understand how they could come along and literally rip a child out of his mother's when there was no evidence to back them up that I was an unfit parent or that my son was at risk of anything other than a mum that at times was a little eccentric.

I never knew what was going to happen next.

Because my mental health was so out of control; I always had to expect the unexpected. DOCS were a big part of both our lives; they checked up on me, called my supports to see if I was attending regular appointments and they even asked me to keep a diary of how I was coping daily that I was expected to show them whenever they asked.

I eventually stopped being honest with my entries because they always twisted everything around. Like one time; after looking through some of the pages they asked me 'you said here that you were really struggling with your little one and didn't feel like you were in control, Are you saying that you can't cope'?

I tried to explain that I actually meant I felt like I couldn't be a mother to my little one because I was afraid that my every move would be scrutinised and picked apart. That I had no confidence in my ability to parent because they had taken him away from me so many times now, that I didn't feel like I was in control of my life.

But they didn't get that. They saw it as me admitting that I wasn't cut out for it and I would rather just give up now and stop trying.

They always wanted to see his bedroom, and watch us play together. I never felt like he was getting the best from me because I was always so on edge and conscious of them hovering in the shadows.

I used to love just snuggling with him on the couch and letting him cuddle up on my knee to watch a dvd; letting him fall asleep in my arms and carry him into his bed. They even turned that into something that it wasn't. Putting into court documents that I was always standing over him, I didn't let him do his own thing.

They said I didn't place boundaries on him or have a set routine.

Every single thing that I did with him was picked apart and made into a big deal. Over time I just stopped with the hugging and letting him sit on my lap for any length of time; because it was easier to deal with.

Do you know how that made me feel?

How those little voices in my head would taunt and tease me, saying 'Hannah we told you that you're not good enough to be his mum' 'he knows that you don't love him anymore' 'he can feel you pushing him away'.

It never stopped!

When I used to put him to bed at night I would sit and cry into the pillow so that he wouldn't hear me. I would cry for hours – wanting to be the mum I was before they turned me into the monster that I had become.

All I wanted to do was curl up beside him and just hold him while he was sleeping and stroke his little face. Listen to him snoring quietly and watch his face as he dreamed.

I couldn't do it!

I wasn't that I didn't want to, I couldn't do it because if I let myself do those things, they would take him away again.

4

In total they took him from me 5 times; the longest was 11 months, 3 weeks and 4 days.

334 nights that I couldn't kiss him goodnight.

334 nights that he has to spend in a strange bed;

334 nights that when he called out for his mummy, it was someone else's mummy that came to him.

334 nights that I cried myself to sleep and fought with the demons in my head that told me to end it all because I couldn't even be a mother to my babies.

I've noticed lately that the wall is still there between us.

I feel myself pulling away from his hugs; fearful that I've held onto him for too long.

When he is upset these days; instead of giving him a hug I try to talk to him and change the subject. This is not the kind of mother I want to be to him!

He got the worst of it out all three of my boys. He was the one that got ripped from my arms so many times that in the end he didn't even cry anymore. He is the one that saw how badly my mental health got. He saw me when I wouldn't move from the bed because my depression was so bad I could barely breathe. And it is him that understands way too much for a child of only 10.

He has seen more than most kids do in their entire childhood and has heard so much pain in his mother's voice, that he can work out how I am simply by saying hello. This pains me. Every day I try to break through that wall, every day I tell myself that I need to be stronger, I need to be braver. But I just can't be that way with him.

Of course this isn't fair to him, but I am trying so fucking hard my heart aches! We have been to therapy together. We've been to therapy separately. But there is just something that stops me from breaking through. I fear that one day he is going to tell me that he hates me for treating him different; and I will say honestly that I don't know how I will react. I know I will say I hate me for it too, but that isn't going to change anything is it?

I have contacted DOCS a few times, asking them to pay for our therapy sessions. After all; it is because of their actions that this is happening. But they don't want to hear from us unless there is something wrong.

My argument is that there was nothing wrong to begin with – but that just falls on deaf ears. As long as I am meeting his needs, they say I am doing what I am supposed to. It's just a pity they didn't think that 7 years ago!! How different our lives would be.

I remember a time, about 6 months after they first took him away; when they called me to ask if I gave permission for him to go with the foster parents to get his hair cut. I told them no, because I was going to have it done next time I had a visit with him. Can you guess what they told me?

I wouldn't be allowed to do that next visit because the worker who would be present didn't have the qualifications to defend herself if I suddenly became unwell and used the scissors as a weapon. I was dumbfounded!

Not only were they totally over reacting, they were uneducated about mental illness! To say that if I 'suddenly became unwell' was so ignorant and damaging.

I don't suffer from schizophrenia or psychosis, and even if I did that statement was so far from fact that I was gobsmacked to say the least! To even make such a stupid statement only confirmed what I already knew to be true. They had no fucking idea what mental illness was, let alone what mine was about.

So after arguing and getting upset at their stupidity, I had to give in and agree to let the foster carers take him for a haircut. When I saw him next I just burst into tears. His haircut was awful; it just wasn't fair.

Yes I know that it was still my baby … but the cut was all wrong. They had shaved off his beautiful curls and he was given a number 5 all over. The cut was horrible. Every time I saw him I was just reminded of their stupidity and ignorance. It's easy to say 'it's just a haircut' but it was more than that. It was a loss of power, a loss of my right to be a mother to him, and a loss of dignity. What mother do you know can't even take her baby to get a haircut or better still do it herself? I don't.

There was also another occasion when their ignorance was very clear to me.

I was scheduled to have 3 hours of supervised access at my new place with him. I was so excited to show him his new room! I had spent hours putting it together and making it look nice for him.

I'd bought him a new doona cover with his favourite cars character on it; made sure his favourite teddies were all lined up along the end of the bed. Had race tracks set up and a big box of shiny new bright blocks. I was so excited to show him. But when they came to my place with him and heard me telling him about his room, they said I wasn't allowed to take him in there until it had been checked.

Excuse me?! What the hell?!

Are you fucking kidding me?!

Checked for what? Weapons.

They wanted to check that I hadn't hidden a knife in the tub of blocks, or a knife under his pillow to attack them with. My god! What the fuck is wrong with these people that they would even think that I would risk my sons safety by hiding a weapon in there or even have the thought cross my mind?!

My little boy couldn't go into his bedroom until they had had their security team come and do a check of the room. A check that upturned all his toys, stripped his bed of his new blanket, and left his room looking like I didn't give a crap about his belongings. How could this even be real?!

I tried to make the most of it, like make the cleaning up and putting everything back into place a game; but I couldn't hold back the tears. Instead of spending the 3 precious hours we had together playing and laughing and being happy; it was spent cleaning up. No child should have to go through that kind of insane, over the top, stupid nonsense! But he did. We did. And when he asked me 'mummy why is my new room all messy? Has somebody been playing with my toys?' I had to lie and tell him that I hadn't had time to do it before he came. And once again I came off as not giving a fuck about him or his things.

Out of everything they put us through in those 2 years, that; and when they ripped him from my arms, remains with me as the most damaging. Fucked up and made no sense then and still doesn't now.

Some days I hate DOCS more than others. Most of the time we can go about our days like normal and laugh, play and enjoy being together. Then there are other days when I notice he is a little quieter than usual because he has remembered something and doesn't want to tell me about it because it might upset me; it is when this happens that I turn to my laptop and I write. I switch off from everything else and go back to then and put it into words. It's the only constructive way I have that works. I still feel like I'm letting him down sometimes.

Taken. What does that mean? The definition of the word is 'remove (someone or something) from a particular place' but it is more than that for me.

My child was taken.

My reason for getting up every day was taken.

My son's innocence about life was taken.

His belief that mummy will always be there for him was taken.

His whole world as he knew it to be at 2 and a half years old, was taken.

The part of me that was there for my son emotionally was taken.

His ability to understand and use his emotions in the right way was taken. Even his tears when he cried were taken!

Because when he was taken to that house full with strangers and left there with nothing and no one that was familiar to him; he cried. They told him that he didn't need to cry because he was going to be okay, and that these people were going to look after him.

But he wasn't okay because in his little messed up mind ... everything that he knew and loved was gone far far away and he was too little to understand that it was only temporary.

From that moment on, he was lost inside his own little head. Too little to understand and too young to make sense of the chaos that had been forced on him.

That was a slice of his life taken.

He wasn't okay and he still isn't 8 years later.

So I think titling the book TAKEN represents more than 'remove (someone or something) from a particular place' and maybe, just maybe we can get some clarity on this sad and lonely time in our lives.

Our memories were taken and replaced with tears, pain, heartache and sadness and for that I am not only sorry but devastated. My little boy lost his mummy that day, she was taken and replaced by a shadow.

Still to this day, he waits for her to come back and put her arms around him and whisper in his ear 'mummy will keep you safe. I will always be here for you' just like she did all those years ago when the house was full of Christmas decorations and the smell of freshly mowed grass was coming in through the windows. He waits and hopes and blames himself for her not being here and at the same time she waits and blames herself and beats herself up over and over again because that isn't who she is anymore. She can't be. It happened so many times in the end that it was easier to put a wall up that protected me from the pain of them taking him away, but I built it up so high that now I don't know how to take it down.

That's Taken.

Just recently I had an argument with a family friend about how I 'lack' compassion towards him sometimes. I appear cold and uncaring towards him in her opinion. I hate hearing things like that.

It is not my intention to be like that and it hurts to think that maybe he feels the same way too; but I just can't do any more than I already am. I just can't.

It doesn't feel right. I love him and I protect him with everything I have in me to keep him safe, and I am so proud of how far he has come since the therapy started.

He has friends now and he has kept the same friend for almost 2 years and he has settled down in school and no longer throws the big tantrums that he used to when he couldn't verbalise how he was feeling. It's a huge change in him and I tell him that I am proud of him all the time. It's like he is a different little boy!

But hearing my friend say those things makes me feel like everything we have been through, all the counselling and family treatment has been for nothing because from the outside it still looks the same. I still look I guess 'robotic' in my movements with him and in my actions.

If you could see inside of me and see my heart when he is around, you will see that it is restricted, almost like it is too painful for it to swell with pride the way it should because after years of having being hurt so many times; it is being cautious and protects itself.

You would see that my muscles are twitching for me to move that bit closer towards him and hold him tighter; you would see that behind my eyes there are tears threatening to fall and that it takes every ounce of my strength not to be consumed by the guilt each and every time he makes me proud. But you can't see all of that and I just look like I'm being a cold, heartless bitch mother.

Oh when will this cycle end?!

Now I think is a good time to fill you in on the lead up to DOCS taking my babies away; because some will argue that it was the right thing to do; while others, such as myself, disagree.

After my marriage fell apart I was lost in my depression. To feel validated and worthy I used pills to numb myself from reality and a few times I took too many pills and needed to go to hospital. When this happened my boys were ALWAYS cared for by a friend. They were in bed, asleep when the ambulance came and if I did need to stay overnight in hospital, then my friend would stay with them until I came back home. Eventually however; the hospital notified DOCS that I had overdosed on pills and they came out to investigate.

At first they were satisfied that the boys were always well cared for and that I had support if I felt that I needed to go to hospital. Six weeks after they came to check up on me and my boys, my mental health deteriorated very badly and I was chronically depressed and unable to look after my boys. I had no other option but to ask DOCS to take my boys and put them in foster care so that I could go to hospital and get the help I needed. Once they collected my boys, I fell apart.

I was admitted to the psychiatric unit and I stayed there for two weeks. I started taking some anti-depressant medication and was feeling more in control of my life.

When I came home, my boys did to.

Things were going along fine until my youngest son's dad became unwell; and when he stopped taking our 2 year old on the weekends the pressure for me was too much. I needed the break, to have things slow down so that my head could catch up.

Those days when it may be silent but your head is so full and chaotic that it sound like there is a party in there, but you have no way of turning down the noise; that's why I needed the break.

Over time I started to get worse and my mental health declined again. The boys went back to the foster carers and I went back into hospital, only this time I didn't respond to treatment as quickly as I had before and instead of them letting me out after 2 weeks, they made me involuntary and DOCS made my boys being in foster care permanent.

This changed everything.

Had I not been sectioned under the Victorian mental health act 1986, I would not be alive today to tell my story. While a patient on the ward I tried to hurt myself at least once a day. I tried using a plastic bag to suffocate myself; I smashed the mirror to use the broken pieces to slash my wrists.

I drank perfume, swallowed another patients medication and I even barricaded myself in the bathroom and tried to hang myself with the bed sheets.

I was intent on ending my life so that my children would forget me and have a normal life without me in it.

I wanted what was best for them, and I was convinced that taking me out of their lives would better it for them.

My battles with DOCS were just beginning and then as if life was saying to me 'you are so screwed' I broke my leg in 2 places.

I broke my tibia and fibia and needed an operation to set the bones in place. I had plaster up to my knee and was in a wheelchair to get around the house.

Once I got out of hospital I thought that I would get my boys back; but DOCS were taking me to court. They were saying that I was a risk to them and that if they stayed with me I was going to hurt them! I was horrified!

I would never ever, ever hurt my boys! No matter how bad life was for me – or what was going on with me, my boys were ALWAYS protected from it. So that is how my battle began with DOCS to get my boys back.

Over the next six months my eldest son was sent to my mother in Tasmania and my 2 year old was in part time foster care. The other times he was with his dad.

It stayed like this for about 4 months; and that was then my ex-husband's health took a turn for the worst and he told DOCS that he could no longer have him in his care.

I had just moved into a nice new place and I was FINALLY out of plaster; my case manager had been to see me that morning and made comment about how well I was.

I had not been in hospital for 4 months (the longest time for me up to this point) and my mood was settled. I was spending more and more time with my little one.

Things were finally looking up!

It was 2.36pm on a Thursday afternoon and I was happy …..and we are back to the beginning of this story.

So … that is the story of what happened before, during and after 2.36pm on that Thursday afternoon and the profound affect that is has had on us all.

What followed was 5 years of fighting to get my eldest son to come back home to be with his younger brother and me; 3 years of fighting to get my little one off the books at DOCS, and a lot of tears in between.

A lot of people pass judgement on what they assume to be fact and others say nothing at all.

I say "know the facts, know the person, know who was involved and why" then you can say whatever the hell you like! But there are some that don't even know about this part of my life; and that's not because I hide it from them, it's just because the conversation hasn't come up and I don't feel the need to explain.

There are some poeple that are real friends. They know there is a reason why sometimes when I answer the door I have tears in my eyes; or that sometimes I don't talk a lot like I usually do. They know there are a million stories I've never told them or anyone else, and they respect me enough not to ask. I might have nothing to write for months at a time, but then just as much to say as ever before.

I don't want to be understood by everyone, I don't even want to be liked. I just want to share a small part of my life journey with you in the hope that something I said has spoken to you.

You can empathise with my pain and understand why I hurt. Had these things not happened to me, I wouldn't be who I am today.

These experiences made me stronger and they challenged me in ways that I've never been before.

I am a better person because of what I have lived through. I'm still working on me; still working on the mum in me that needs to let down that wall so my son can get through.

There are days when thinking about all of this brings me to tears and I can't bear the thought of not being here for me boys! But I realise that it will all take time and that I'm lucky enough now to have that, because there was a time when I could not see the future.

I never had plans for the weekend, never planned to visit anyone. All I could do was exist from day to day and make it through as best I could.

Making plans for a future I didn't believe in made no sense to me; and waking up was a curse.

What would you do if someone took your everything away and told you to find a reason to get up tomorrow?

How would you react if the court system told you that you couldn't go to hospital for 12 months or you couldn't have your children back?

Society needs to get educated about mental illness!

You wouldn't tell someone with cancer that you would take their children away if you went into hospital for treatment would you? Having a mental illness is exactly the same. NOT getting treatment when you need it may kill you – the same with cancer.

These days it is a lot harder for DOCS to take children away from their parents; especially if they have a mental illness. I would like to say that I had helped to get this system changed; but I can't.

I can however say that I am helping to change the system of mental health and I'm helping to educate others that are fighting their own battles. For now that will have to be enough.

9

I gave everything I had to mental illness and still it asked for more!

When I was in a heap on the bathroom floor barely breathing from the pain, it still wanted more. When there was so much noise inside my mind that it felt the entire world was screaming at once, still it wanted more.

If I dared to smile at my reflection in the mirror, the demons in my mind would taunt and poke fun at me, pointing out my flaws like numbers called in a race.

One after the other the voices took turns to tear me down, leaving me scarred and skin so broken and raw; the slightest breeze would cause me to break down and cry.

When I woke up in the mornings and tried to start the day, even if I had slept for 20 hours the day before – a darkness of tiredness would come and cover me. It would wrap me inside its lying arms and promise to make it safe for me to stay inside. It always took so much strength to break free from deep inside. Even when I gave my life; still it wanted more!

For those 3 minutes when I was on the edge of life and death, it teased me and taunted me with promises of protection when really it wanted to keep up its cruel torture of pain.

So it sent me back. Back to live more of its sickening hell.

Every time I sliced my skin, it would tell me it wasn't deep enough. When I dared to try and fight back; my energy would be short lived, because like a snake's venom it would slowly invade my body and suck the life from inside of me. No matter how hard my body cried out in pain from endless nights of torture, still it wanted more.

Standing in the shower while the blood ran from my skin, mixing like a watery drink of poison was never quite enough. It had to take the strength from within my legs and have me begging for mercy on my knees.

When at last it gave me a break from everything it did to me, I could breathe like it was my first time! Huge gulps of air I would suck into my tired lungs and the more air I sucked in me the stronger I would feel!

I started getting feeling in my fingers for the first time in what felt like forever and I had colour back in my cheeks that had been white for so long. But the cruel joke would soon become clear as the deep breaths of air turned into me fighting to keep it in as it pushed it out of me.

I would hyperventilate and be left gasping like I couldn't remember how to breathe; and it was true. It was taking that bitter sweet air back from me by force!

The cycle was never ending and I ended up craving for sleep to be my only friend. At least while I was sleeping I didn't have to fight with the demons anymore.

There were times when 2 days would turn into 4 before I woke up to realise the demons were stronger than before.

The sleep had given them time to rest and get their energy back. It's like they used the time to revive!

Then I would fight it, sleep was no longer a safe place to be. I only let myself close my eyes for a few moments at a time. It never stopped fighting me, it never stopped taking from me like it was owed some kind of debt.

When I woke up in I.C.U after my suicide attempt; it felt like it knew it had lost its power. Don't get me wrong, it still tried to keep taking from me but now I was able to fight back. Harder! And stronger than I did before.

My struggles became less and I found a way to get through each day that didn't end with me bleeding, scarred or crying out in pain. We came to a deal – a compromise that had us both fighting for the same thing. There was still a power struggle; and IS still a war waging inside me that will no doubt start up again someday, but I am the leader of this fight now! If my demons decide to wake up to fight another day they better be prepared!

I am NOT my mental illness!

I am a warrior!

I am a survivor!

I am free to be who I am meant to be!

I choose to let my demons occupy my mind, but I am the one in control now, and if they dare to try and make life a living hell – I will go into battle! Only this time, it will be THEIR blood that is spilled!

Until next time,

H xx

Nothing held back the tears when he told me the terrible things that they say when they think he's gone far away. I felt the pain of his tears as he cried on my shoulder about how much he misses his daddy.

He told me he wished that he could be angry at him for going away and not waiting for him to grow up. He said 'why couldn't he wait for me to make him proud?' it didn't matter that I said he WAS already proud of him, from the moment he was born.

He said he was too little then to hear him when he whispered it in his ear. When he misses him more; I hear him calling out to him when he sleeps … 'daddy where are you? Daddy where did you go?' and all I can do is lay in bed and let my tears sink into the pillow and cry for him.

When I get up tomorrow I wait for him to tell me he dreamed about his daddy and act like it I wasn't crying the night before when I heard him call his name.

I love all three of my boys and they will always be my babies, not matter how big they grow. I have a different relationship with each of them, I am a different "mum" depending who I am with.

My eldest; now 18 – copped a lot a crap when I was unwell, but when he went to live with his grandmother he was protected from a lot that my now 10 year old experienced.

He had to call another mum and have her do the things that I never got to do. When he cried out at night when he was scared; it wasn't me that came.

It's like he had to grow up so fast that he never got to be the little boy he was meant to be. He can read me now; knows when I have too much on my mind or when I having nothing left to say. He takes the job of 'man of the house' a little too literally some times, and forgets that he isn't meant to be the one taking the bins away when they are full.

I have come to expect a lot from him – not always a good thing given he is still only 10 years old.

When I remember the things I've asked him to do I am overcome with guilt and try to undo what I have done.

I didn't make the connection that he was fighting a battle at school when he was always cranky and moody. I just assumed that it was me that he had a problem with, but didn't want to upset me and tell me about it.

This time though; it wasn't me. It was a horrible little boy in his class that was making his life a living hell!

The things this child would say just to bring him to tears, only to then tease him for crying about it!

When he couldn't keep it to himself any longer and he finally let me see how much it hurt him, I felt like I had let him down. Why had I not seen that he was hurting? Am I so out of tune with him that I couldn't feel his pain like he can see mine when it's written all over my face? What was wrong with me?!

What I would do to have that time with him again. I would be stronger and I wouldn't let them take him away!

TIMS POEM

When the system took my babies away
And they left me crying on the floor,
You were the one that stayed behind
And didn't throw me out the door

Your support and encouragement is like no one else
Please believe it's true,
You treat us better than my family does
Because they have left me,
Black and blue.

My boys admire you for who you are
And all you stand to be,
I'm so proud to call you a lifelong friend
And I want the world to see.

The things that you have done for us
Are amazing,
Phenomenal
And true.
You're always there to cheer us on,
Telling us that we can be strong
And even when I'd lost all hope
You showed me even more ways to cope.

We've always needed an angel
And I'm so glad that we have you
To help us when the road gets touch
You know exactly what to do.

Even when I tried to quit
You wouldn't have a bar of it
You kept me focused
You kept me strong
Even when it all went wrong.

Our lives are so much richer
In every way that it can be
In you I can see everything
That I would want my boys to be.

You're an extra special person
Truly one of a kind
And if no one else can see that
Then they really must be blind.

Knowing you is making our lives
A better,
Happier,
Brighter
Place to be.

Thank you for being our hero.

Thinking in Black and White

Black and white thinking is so typical of BPD. Everything is either all good or everything is either all bad. There is no in between.

Classic behavior when things are bad is to fall apart and be in a state of crisis where intervention is needed to keep the person safe. Just acknowledging their pain and give them the space to vent, cry or scream. Because usually; once they have worked it through – they are fine and 'over it' so to speak.

I remember when I was pregnant with my youngest son how this black and white thinking affected my every move! It had a lot to do with the baby's father, but I remember feeling so 'out of control of my life' but not 'out of control of me'. It was exhausting!

My case manager at the time just didn't get it! She was more of a hindrance than a help. Like the time I told her I felt like I was living someone else's life ... and she tried to put me into hospital! Her reasoning was she felt that I was disassociating and at risk of harm. However; as I mentioned earlier ... this WAS NOT the case because I needed to 'feel' in order to hurt myself.

So... I used to fake my way through our sessions. I pretended to be okay so that she would leave me alone. I cried when she wasn't around. I screamed when no one was listening and I made her believe that my relationship troubles were a thing of the past.

And speaking of relationships ... THEY WERE HARD! In so many ways they were exhausting and painful.

Friendships were always tested to the point of no return, and when it was all over – the guilt would have a go at us too. I forgave people simply because I didn't want to be alone. I gave out chance after chance after chance just to keep someone else happy. They would treat me like crap and I would let them. The saying 'it's better to have someone than it is to have no one' is true when you have BPD.

After the first dozen or so times of failing to maintain a significant friendship, you learn to realize that the only way for you to not get hurt ... is for you to be the one doing the hurting. So using, abusing, and relying on friends to keep you safe became a habit hard to break.

Many people left when they couldn't take it anymore. They couldn't understand how you can be okay while they are there with you, but within hours of them leaving you were a mess and contemplating suicide because the thought of being alone terrified you!

Then there is the relationship with my mother!

She always made me feel like a failure. At every opportunity she would tell me and anyone who would listen how disappointed in me she was. She pointed out my flaws and mocked me when I cried, and it was such a regular thing for her to do and my way of coping was to hurt myself.

The first time I took out the razor blade and cut myself I was 11 years old. At first my fingers shook as I cut but when I got that overwhelming sense of relief it became easier to do. As I grew up I didn't do it as much, and not because I didn't need to! I had just found other ways of coping

I got pregnant at 17 and I think it was at this point that I came to realize that she hated me. She was jealous of me and no matter what I did, it was never good enough! Even while I was in labour she was barking out orders and telling me what to do.

Looking back now, I can see the signs of depression in her. She never got help for it, and when I started seeing a psychologist for post-natal depression, it was just another reason for her to mock me.

If I could go back to my 18 year old self – I would tell her it doesn't matter! All of the heartache of the past won't matter in 15 years' time. What your mother thinks about you doesn't matter because you are going to be a great mother to your children and you will be nothing like her. But at the time any relationship was worth the pain I had to endure to keep it, no matter how long it lasted.

The best advice I can give to anyone who has BPD; is to accept it as part of who you are and stop fighting it. Because once you do that, you will begin to understand who it is you are meant to be.

To anyone supporting a loved one with BPD I say never stop trying. We don't do the things we do to hurt you, all we want is to know that no matter what you love us and will always be there to support us.

For those that work with us and try to help us learn to understand ourselves ... thank you. It's not your job to love us, or stick with us when it gets too hard but you do. And for that ... there is nothing more that can be said except thank you.

Having BPD and being a single parent – I have to remind myself that when I am having a tough day, that it's okay for my boys to see me cry and feel like shit. I don't hide my BPD from them, because if I did that, I would be teaching them to hide how they feel. I want them to understand that it is okay to NOT be okay, that is passes, and as long as you give yourself the time to go through the motions, then you will be feeling better again soon.

Having BPD also means that my emotions are always on high alert. Because we can't regulate our moods and emotions, it's like we are always on hyper alert. We question everything we feel and overthink it. We sit and question why we question the question.

When we cry we react with anger and frustration; because we didn't want to cry in this situation; we wanted to feel the hurt and not react, but our brains aren't not wired like that.

Understanding how to regulate moods and reactions take a lot of blood, sweat and tears. It needs to happen by choice NOT force. If you are not ready to accept your diagnosis, then you are not ready to accept treatment.

If I went to a counsellor or psychiatrist and they asked me how I was feeling, I would look at them and say "I don't know", because I didn't. Most of the time I never had a clue what it was I was feeling at any given moment because my body was so used to being in a state of high tension that a normal feeling wasn't a normal thing to feel.

I've sat many hours in a room with a doctor or case worker and talked about everything from how many loads of washing I had done that week, or if I should go home and mop the kitchen floor. But I couldn't tell them how I was feeling! That may be a simple question to them … but to me, they may as well have asked me to explain the physics of human life! It was THAT complex!

I used to disassociate a lot when I was very unwell. My body would shut down and go through the motions. But I didn't feel anything because what was happening in my head was too hard to understand. I have been put into psych wards many times when this has happened, because they said I was at risk of hurting myself. I appeared to be vacant and uncaring, and I was, but I wouldn't have hurt myself because one thing I have come to understand about having BPD is I can't hurt myself if I'm not there to feel it. I needed to feel the pain, otherwise it wasn't going to happen. Pain made me feel alive. Disassociation didn't allow that to happen.

Sometimes when my workers told me that I was coming across as unresponsive or challenging or difficult, I was actually in survival mode. It wasn't a conscious thing that happened, like, I couldn't CONTROL it, it just crept up on me and even if I was aware of it, it wasn't in my control to fix. When workers said this I would usually miss a few sessions. It was easier to do that than to explain myself.

Again.

Having BPD makes me who I am today. I know how it feels to be the only one fighting at 3am; how scared I was when the pills I took started to slowly kill me from the inside. How I felt when the image of my sons went flashing before my eyes as the darkness came to cover me.

BPD has made me question everything in my life and scrutinize it to within an inch of my existence. It took years of my life from me and still tries to take from me today; but now I am stronger because of what it has done to me. I gave it all of myself and won.

I didn't know how to live with BPD and I didn't want anything to do with it! Eventually it demanded my attention and I had no choice but to face it, learn its weaknesses and find a way to co-exist together.

At first I saw no point in listening to the voice of 'me' in my head, after all it never had anything nice to say. But that was the point. I needed to listen to it – and challenge that thinking.

So when I stood in front of the mirror and the voice started pointing out my flaws, I would say in a firm voice that I liked the way my hair looked today or I liked the way I smiled. It felt weird, I felt stupid and I never thought that it would make an ounce of difference! But after 3 weeks of doing this every time I saw a reflection of myself it became second nature. I was unconsciously retraining that part of my brain. I didn't hear the voice anymore – or maybe I was so used to challenging it that eventually it just gave up trying to ruin me.

I noticed that I also liked to make jokes about myself, not always nice, by way of reflecting others away from perhaps noticing that I was different. So I challenged myself to stop doing that. Made a deal with myself that if I stopped cracking jokes at my own expense, I would start putting more effort into looking nice. My current wardrobe at the time was all black; so anything had to be an improvement right?!

This gave me confidence. I hadn't realized it before, but I had zero self-esteem. When stress of life became too much to handle I used to do anything to make that ball of anxiety go away! Drinking, smoking, drugs, speeding, putting myself in dangerous positions in which I could have died or been seriously injured. So I stopped drinking and smoking, even stopped smoking pot and the money I saved from giving up these dirty habits got me into a course. I had no intentions of finishing! Saw it simply as a distraction, but I finished and I passed.

Challenging myself became a new obsession. The part inside me that said I couldn't do something was silenced every time I succeeded.

Learned behaviour is easy to do, but hard to conquer. I learnt fast that if I overdosed on pills and went to hospital, I would be accepted at my worst and I would have people there telling me I was worthy of the treatment because I was unwell and it wasn't my fault. That soon became a regular pattern. I only took enough so I needed to go to hospital, never enough to kill myself. I would always have so much guilt after, because once it was over I felt like an idiot! But I needed that validation so much that in the moment of doing it, I could rationalize it in my mind. It was too insignificant to matter.

This pattern of learned behaviour wasn't always on a subconscious level of knowing what I was doing. It was a negative action that caused a positive reaction – and it was easy to become addicted. I needed to know that someone cared about me. Someone wanted me to get better. Someone believed in me. That I was a good enough person to help. Breaking that addiction was the hardest and took the most out of me emotionally.

I used to believe that the only way I could control myself was to be on medication. It was like a placebo effect that, once I had swallowed the pills, I would 'feel better' and I would convince myself I would be okay. And if I forgot to take my meds I would panic! Work myself into a state by over scrutinizing my every move and thinking the entire time oh my god my hands are shaking so that means I am not okay … when it reality my hands were shaking because I was in the middle of a breakdown and it was normal for that to happen. Again, this was learned behaviour that would end up needing crisis intervention.

If you suffer from BPD and you tell someone you have a mental illness, it's like they don't hear the Borderline when you say BPD and they go oh so how many of you are there? IGNORANT PEOPLE! Then when you try to explain it, they just look away, too stupid to understand that turning away makes you feel like crap.

I liked to exaggerate things too, little things became big things and this would get me attention so I kept doing it. Silly now when I look back but at the time it felt perfectly normal to build up the story to make it sound better. Most of the time it wasn't a lie, so it never hurt anyone. I talk to people with BPD and I can tell when they are doing this to me, and I let them finish the story, but then I change the subject. That too is learned behaviour because at some point in time I told a story that got some attention or some follow up and that then made me unconsciously fall into the habit of inflating a story.

I remember when my case worker told me this, I exploded! How dare you call me a liar! How dare you tell me I am making up stories! It was like I was a child that had been found fibbing about something. Truth be told …. That was exactly what I was doing.

Behaving like a small child for attention or to get noticed is EXACTLY what BPD is. You behave like a child because this is the only way our brain knows how to react to a situation that you can't handle.

Almost like we never got to be children but we are expected to grow up and be adults. That shit is just way too hard!

Here lies the retraining of your brain. You need to learn how to use your emotions correctly, use your anger for when you are angry. Cry when you are sad, scared, lost, frustrated. Laugh when you are happy, nervous or amused. But as simple as that sounds … to us it is extremely hard to regulate.

As young children we learnt from an early age to show no emotion; to hold everything in. Because if you let it out you were punished or mocked, singled out, teased, laughed at or abused. This taught us to hide how we were feeling and to lie about how we felt. We taught ourselves to be quiet and hold everything in and when it got to be too much, we had a breakdown. Parents called it attention seeking when all it really was, was craving for love, support, attention and guidance. Most of us never got that and as a result of that behaviour we grow up to have BPD.

I see BPD traits in my own child. It breaks my heart and I think hang on … I didn't do anything wrong! Why does he have it??

Then I remember that he HAS had significant trauma in his life. DOCS took him away from me when I was unwell. They assumed that I could damage him more than their system would.

THEY WERE WRONG!!!

It is BECAUSE of them taking him away and separating him from his older brother that has made him now question his feelings, reactions emotions and his self as a person.

Fortunately for him, I am unlike my own mother and can see when he is struggling. Rather than ignore it and punish him for feeling the way he does, I can talk to him and together we can work through it. Friends tell me 'he is just like you' and it's hard to hear, because I don't want him to be like me. I want him to be his own person who has a great life full of happiness. But being like me means he will go through life questioning everything, second guessing himself and wondering what the hell he ever did to be the way he is!

And he will …. Because that's what I do.

Part of me still lives back in Tasmania, crying in the corner while no one is looking – waiting for my mother to start yelling at me for one thing or another.

And that's the 12 year old me that wishes someone would come and take her away and love me like all my friends mums seemed to do, even when they did something wrong. I hope that Thomas never feels like that!!

Having BPD makes me a better parent to all of my boys; and for that I am grateful, and I do embrace BPD. I research all the latest info, and I try to better their lives and that of others so that they too can learn to embrace the parts of them that make BPD a bonus.

I did a short course of DBT (Dilectal Behaviour Therapy - retraining your brain so that it responds differently to stress) – and while I was doing it I used to think 'what a load of bullshit! This is not going to make things easier, it will just be harder' and for a long time it was.

It wasn't until I was in hospital after another overdose, that I realized that I was putting those skills into practice and I didn't even know it! I must have been absorbing the information. It has been a longer time between hospital admissions too. It hurts emotionally and physically to understand yourself. It hurts to retrain your brain. It makes you hate BPD even more. But it works. I'm living proof of that.

Teaching ourselves how to get a positive reaction from a negative situation can be deadly.

Craving validation can make us do some pretty unhealthy and risky things. I used to crave attention of any kind; good or bad and I got it any way I could. It wasn't a matter of putting effort into it or making a plan; most of the time it was happening before I realised it and before I knew it I was out of control.

Most of the time I got the attention from hospital staff after I turned up in the emergency department after an overdose. Only a small one, nothing that was going to do much other than make me sleep; but after a while even that 'novelty' wore off and the staff got sick of seeing me there all the time.

I've had to teach myself that it is much healthier to 'get a positive reaction to a positive action' and that it isn't as hard as it sounds.

Firstly start paying attention to what you tell yourself, because you are listening. Start by finding one thing about yourself that you like. It may only be small, but it is a focus point. Then every day try to add one more thing to the list, so that when the negative voice in your head start pointing out your faults; you start by listing the positives. Say it loud enough and often enough that in time; you won't even hear that negative voice.

Much better than trying to drown out that negativity with alcohol or drugs and do it yourself for free.

When I am having a 'sook' over something and just can't seem to stop crying, I go and watch myself in the mirror. No one likes to see themselves cry; and in my case, I will start laughing and mock myself and soon enough I will have forgotten what I was crying about.

Only little things, and it might not work for everyone but you never know unless you try!

Remember all those times when you promised yourself that next time when you see the warning signs that you would get help? Remember the deals you made with yourself that you have broken so many times lately that you have lost count of them? When the darkness enveloped you within its arms and promised to keep you safe, do you remember the how quickly you started to believe in its lies?

Now, this very moment is hard to take in. My fingers are shaking as they search for the keys to make the words and my knees are trembling with fear; but I am sitting down.

There is darkness everywhere I look around these days. Even when the sun is shining outside I feel cold and empty. Like something inside me is gone and I don't know what it is exactly, so I can't even begin to try and find it.

I cry a lot at the moment. Not just a few tears that slide down my face, it's the big crocodile tears that tear me apart and leave me gasping for breath on my knees.

There is no one thing that triggers them, they just start and I can't make them stop. Even now; I have to stop and take a deep breath because they are there, shining brightly in my eyes enough that I can barely see the screen. It's been so long since I've been here; but at the same time it feels so familiar that years seem like only days. I've done all the things I have in the past to look after myself, but they don't seem to work anymore.

Would it be too much if I were to say I feel like I'm drowning but I'm nowhere near the water? It's like I'm confined inside a box that follows me wherever I go but no one else can see it. They just see me when I walk past.

I went to see my doctor, and he can see that it's covering me and trying to lure me further, deeper inside.

He gave me medication to help take the anxiety and paranoia away and I know I should take it … but then I feel like I've given up in defeat. I should be stronger than this! I WAS stronger than this. What happened? When did it all become so overwhelming and hard to exist as I am in the world?

My babies keep me fighting. They are the reason I hang on. But it's not their job to make me want to stay; I've got to want to stay for me. Tonight I want to stay, to wake tomorrow to fight another day; and even though the tears have slipped out from behind my eyelids and started racing down my cheeks, I still want to stay.

When does it start to make sense again? I'm lonely, but don't want anyone near me to see it all. I can have friends come visit for hours and I've literally got nothing to say. The conversations I'm having are not with them; they are in my head and it's hard to concentrate on anything they have to say. But from the moment they leave and I've shut the door; I want to scream out for them to come back, to not leave me alone anymore.

I used to try and dress nice everyday so that I could go out and at least 'look normal' to the rest of the world; but today I left home without brushing my hair or changing into clean clothes that weren't splattered with paint. I looked like I felt. A mess. I was one of 'those people' that we all tend to want to steer clear of when you're out in public.

The 'weirdos' that could crack at any given moment over the tiniest little thing, and start yelling at everyone around them. And you know what? That's exactly how I felt! Like I was going to explode.

Some may say I didn't do anything today; but I got up even when my head was telling me no. I managed to cook a decent meal for my children even though I wasn't going to eat any of it. And I took myself to the doctor and I told him I'm not okay.

Yes the laundry is still waiting to be washed and the dishes are still piled up on the sink. And the floor still has that sticky spot from where my toddler spilt juice a couple of days ago … but I don't care about any of that. It is just too much for me to deal with, it overwhelms me and then my anxiety kicks in again. It may all still be there this time next week; but I am doing this one day at a time and right now tomorrow doesn't matter. I've got to get through this night first. And that it a battle I hope I can win, because the consequence of giving into those negative thoughts that are screaming in my head are too much for me to bear.

You might call me weak for being so real, so raw with what it's like to be in this moment right now; but that only shows your ignorance. Not mine.

I need help to get me through this tunnel and out the other side. It hurts to breathe, it hurts to cry, and it hurts me to see my children suffer because their mummy is fighting a war they have no idea about.

I'm a mummy who loves her babies and wants to be here for them tomorrow.

Writing this down helps me quieten the voices a little inside. Writing means that deep inside this dark cloud is the Hannah that kicks ass when she sees someone she cares about hurting. I know she is in here ... please won't you come back out now? Remind me how I can find her. Remember the promises you made all those years ago? You won't let this darkness consume you forever; so come back Hannah. Come back! I need you.

The night has only been here for a few short hours, but it's already been here too long. I need the morning light to give me hope for tomorrow.

I won't let this win.

I'm just waiting this out so that when it finally starts to weaken the hold it has on me; I can break free and live again.

Why, when we feel like crap, does our mind decide that it too needs to be a bully? It replays our saddest moment, our mistakes and out heartaches like a friggen movie stuck on rewind!

Why can't it just leave us with the good stuff? Something to make us feel better instead of joining in and making us feel even worse than we did before.

I have been having a really hard time this week with my health. I feel like my body is fighting me from the inside and it refuses to let up!

Then; as if out of torment, my brain kicks into high gear and starts playing the sad twisted errors of my past mistakes. Do you have any idea how hard it is to FIGHT right now?

My entire body is screaming at me to just give up, and I am trying. I mean REALLY, REALLY trying to not listen to it … but I keep thinking what the fuck am I still fighting for?!

It will be like this tomorrow when I wake up, and the next day and then the next.

My body will scream out in pain the moment I wake up, and my head will start up with the bullshit just like it did today.

When I get like this I am a horrible person! I am moody and nasty, I'm angry and sad at the same time.

I don't know what will make me feel better or how to stop being this bitchy psycho woman that hates everyone almost as much as she hates herself.

I need to invest in some tape that reads 'Approach with caution' and wear it as a sash across my chest, so that if anyone looks at me the wrong way and cops a mouthful, they can't say they weren't warned!

If this is going to be 'life' from now on … then I think its okay to call BULLSHIT!

BULLSHIT is this fun!

BULLSHIT is this normal!

BULLSHIT is this hell worth living over and over again every single day!

So what happens now?

I wish I knew but I don't.

When you were drowning,
I held you up.
When you couldn't focus,
I took the lead.
When you were hurting,
I took the pain away.
When darkness was your only friend,
I held a torch for you.
When I need a friend to talk to,
I couldn't talk to you.
When I was lost and confused,
I tried looking for you,
When I needed a life line,
I had trouble getting through.
When I felt like I was losing,
I cried out for you.
Finally when I caught up with you,
And I asked you for some help.
You gave me a deadly look
That made my legs just melt.
I guess I wasn't anything,
Especially not a friend.
Because why else would you give me rope,
With an anchor on the end?

Why Do I Write?

Writing is like a drug that frees me from the haunting thoughts in my mind that keep me awake at night. Once free - they bring peace to my soul and allows me the freedom to tame the monsters that live inside.

Have you ever tried to be someone you're not just to please someone else? Did you allow yourself to be treated less than you deserve because you wanted someone else to be happy? Have you cried more times than you can remember, for the same reason, because of the same person? Do you tell yourself never again? But you always let them back in to treat you the same as always? Do you stop to ask yourself why?

I did, but I never said it loud enough that my heart could hear. It always came out like a whisper and I let someone take away parts of me that I've had to learn to live without.

Don't get me wrong. I have grown and learnt from living with only half of who I once was, and knowing what I do now; it has all made me a stronger better version of myself.

They say what doesn't kill you only makes you stronger and I for one believe that this is true!

When you are fighting every single day of your life to be treated equal in a society that seems determined to break anything it feels is not 'normal', finding the courage and strength to advocate for yourself is extremely hard to do. Next time you feel that it's all too much and you want to run away from it all, ask yourself; are you running because of reason? Or are you running because of circumstance?

They are two very powerful, yet different things. Step outside your comfort zone a little and stick up for yourself! Because you are worth the noise, and the time and the energy it takes for someone else to have to listen.

And you might also find in the process a little more determination to make them sit down and start paying attention!

Getting in the way of someone trying to better their life is not something I choose to do. However; when I know the person and can see that the path they are choosing to follow will only end in heartbreak, then I will intervene.

If you can't handle your life as it is right now; you struggle to find time for those important to you and sacrifice happiness for obligation, then … YOU NEED TO SIMPLIFY YOUR LIFE.

Adding another person into your already complicated life is not fair to you or the new addition that you are hoping will help make your life less complicated.

How can you better yourself when you are being weighed down by the past? How can you be a better parent if you sacrifice quality of time for quantity?

When a pattern emerges in behavior that is toxic and detrimental to a person's wellbeing, what kind of friend would I be by not saying anything?

The pattern of behavior always leaves them in a dangerous position where they shut down, and want to continually sleep. They stop eating and they close everyone out that tries to help them when it gets too much. They really should seek psychiatric help; but they don't and it's friends and family that is left to pick up the pieces.

I normally wouldn't say this to anyone, especially someone who needs help, but ENOUGH! There comes a point in your own life that you realize that some people can't be saved. No matter what you do or say to them, they will continue their toxic cycle. Sometimes to save your own mental health, you have to cut them off.

Doing that does not make you a bad person! It means that you respect yourself enough to walk away from a situation that will leave YOU hurt, confused and weak from the fight. Why pour all your energy into helping someone who doesn't want to be helped?

I don't want to sound heartless; because I am actually a really nice person, but I have held so many people up in the past that I've nearly drowned myself.

I put my own life on hold for them. I sat with them, cooked and cleaned for them. Took them to the doctor and dragged them out of the house in the hope that they would feel the sunshine or find a reason to move on. But it always ended in tears.

MINE.

Frustration and helplessness would leave me hurt too.

This is why it is okay to walk away – because it's obvious that they don't respect you, so you need to respect yourself! It isn't always a bad thing to say goodbye, and it will hurt you, but in the end YOU are important too. We can only hope that they learn to see the vicious cycle for themselves and make serious GOOD changes in their life, but until they do ... holding them up while you drown in the aftermath isn't healthy for you either.

Let go.

Depression Is a Liar

Depression is a liar. It is a fake. It is only out to please its own selfish needs and when it gets what it wants; the damage left behind takes years to repair. And if not repaired, then dealt with as best as it can be.

When depression is part of your life; it gets hard to go about your day. It lays with you in your bed and keeps you warm; but when you attempt to get up and start the day, it snuggles in closer and whispers in your ear 'stay here, its safe'.

So you listen and just turn over and go back to sleep.

When you're going about your daily life with fear hidden behind your smile, it threatens to make an appearance and fuck up your day.

You try hard to ignore its lies and the effort put into fighting makes you weaker and weaker. It keeps whispering in your ear that if you do what it tells you, it will stop making you feel so tired all the time.

It judges everything you do. It mocks your efforts when you stand at the mirror to do your hair; it laughs when you put on your makeup and tells you that no one will notice anyway. It fakes concern for you when the anxiety gets to be too much; whispers 'you don't have to tell them that I'm here, I promise to make this feeling go away if you tell them I'm not here'...but it only says that because it knows that once they know that depression is part of your life, they will help you to take it away.

It's like a ghost that haunts you every minute of every day.

It makes the simple things hard to do, and makes you feel inadequate and unseen by those around you.

When you get some reprieve from its constant demands and are able to laugh with your friends and forget about it for a little while; it will hold it against you and makes you pay with everything you've got.

When you get into bed tonight, it will kick-start your brain into going over every stupid decision you have ever made in your life and it will still be replaying at 4am. Then when the alarm goes off at 7am, it will envelope you in its embrace and tell you that you can stay right here today; it will leave you alone as long as you stay and keep it warm by sleeping with the ghost.

It is a battle that is fought every day by millions of people in the world. Many will fail and give in to its lies by sleeping the day away, rather than fighting it off by continuing on.

It effects one in every 4 people; and if you think that no one you know suffers from it then look harder.

Look at how hard those around you are pretending to be okay, they don't want to let others see them struggle, because they already feel so weak. Watch the light in their eyes when they laugh and see if it stays long after the joke is over, or is it gone just as quickly as it came. That could be a sign that someone is fighting a battle you know nothing about.

Sometimes all it takes is for someone to walk up to you and say 'I can see that you are hurting, and I'm here to help you if I can'. That will tell them that their ghost is no longer unseen by those around them.

I hated to let people know that I was being plagued by depression. If I had taken an overdose or ended up in hospital, I never told anyone where I had been. I was too embarrassed, and it wasn't until I wrote my first book that those that knew me knew that I had tried to suicide.

In my case; I felt ashamed that I hadn't been strong enough to fight with my depression and I was scared of what people were going to say. I didn't want sympathy. I didn't want praise for surviving.

I wanted understanding. That's why it is so important if you see someone struggling to help them. Try to understand how they feel and what they are going through; and the conversations they will have will no longer be so one sided. It will empower them to fight! It will let them know that depression is nothing to be ashamed of. Depression is the enemy - not them.

Everyone is different. Some will shout it to the rooftops that depression is a part of their life; others will show you their scars and be proud of them because it shows that they have won. Whatever it takes, is what depression asks of us ... and whatever it takes WE WILL FIGHT IT!

Breathing

Take a deep breath and hold it in.

When there is no more room in your lungs to keep holding it in; close your eyes and let it out slowly. Only small bits at a time.

That feeling you get when you're again free to breathe normally? That's how we feel when someone reaches out their hand to us. Like, finally...it's time to breathe again!

Love who you are, be proud of how far you have come and remember to thank yourself for being the amazing person that you are.

Tomorrow

When I think about tomorrow; I wish today away.

No more feeling lost inside a mind that never slows down. No more faking a smile so that no one stops and asks me am I okay. No more hiding away my tears when they break through the walls. I'm tired of lying to those around me. Telling them I'm okay, when inside my flag is waving. SURRENDER! SURRENDER! Can't anybody see??

We all need someone when the world gets too tough. Your world becomes a bully that knows where to hurt you most. I am not strong enough to keep my demons away, I don't want to fight today. Can I rise above this pain and crash down these confining walls? Will there be somebody, anywhere that can come and watch over me?

My feet are stuck to the ground and I'm finding it hard to move. I'm in too deep! Pull me out from inside my mind; bring me back to some reality. Make my eyes connect with yours. Give me focus for tomorrow; I feel that it is just too far away. It's a promise that I just can't seem to forget. Tomorrow the sun will again rise without any effort from me; does that mean that my mood will also rise? I will somehow feel again what 'normal' is meant to be?

Earphones is my ears and the music takes me away from the chaos that's inside me. A temporary relief from the demons that have awoken and started to torture me. I will believe the words in every song and believe the music when it takes me away.

I don't want to turn it down, I can't hear them laughing at me when the music is like this. They kind of sound like they are drowning, and I can almost be convinced that I am going to be okay again when I wake up tomorrow.

When is my body going to give up and fall asleep? So many false promises! Like, when I wake this will all be forgotten, it will all feel like a dream. The word nightmare fits better for this moment in life. I pinched myself I AM still awake!

I'm always crying when it hurts like this. Feeling like the walls are closing in around me and the chaos and noise in my head makes it hard to hear the world breathe. What did I do? Is this just a challenge that I need to conquer so that I can move on? WHAT IS THIS?!

Tomorrow. There's that word again! Tomorrow. It's not now; it's not yesterday. Not the day after next. Tomorrow. It promises so much but it never arrives, it is always a day away. You don't wake up and say it's tomorrow! Can I catch it if I try harder? It's haunting me ... this word that means so very much. Does relying on something that never eventuates make me mad? Is this meant to make sense...tomorrow? Everything that I am fighting with today will be gone when I reach tomorrow.

When I realized what was happening; rather than bracing myself for the fight I just let my demons wake. Don't ask me why because I don't know!

If tomorrow can do so much more than today can, why does it seem so, so, so far out of reach.

So many questions today that I have no answers for and no doubt so many more tomorrow too; I'm praying for a miracle now. Can this war be won by me? Or have I already been defeated?

Strangers we may be, yet we understand each other more than those here with me in the room. Do you also feel that tomorrow has a lot to answer for???

There are parts of me that no one knows. I have seen, heard and felt more than even I can remember!

People walk in to our lives while we journey through it; and you think that you know who they are. You laugh with them, cry with them, and tell each other secrets that you've never shared before. You just assume that this person, this life that they are leading, is who they are. Who they have always been. No need to think otherwise is there?

But what if the person you now call a friend, let you in on a part of her life that just blows you away and leaves you wondering who they really are? Can you embrace this part of them like you have all the others? Or is it too much of a shock for you to take, and the perception of them is now so warped that you can't shake that feeling this is too much?!

Welcome to my life!

I have friends that have joined me in life and come in at chapter 96 and accepted me as I am, no questions asked. Other have joined me at chapter 42, 55, 78 and 90; and each of them knows a little more than the one that came in before.

I recently opened up to some friends about a part of my life they never ever knew about; told them about what I had gone through in a time before I knew them. Some of them have accepted what I did and said and we have been able to continue on with our friendship just like before. They have a better understanding about why I am the way I am with certain situations and are more aware of my limits.

Then there are others that have just shut me down emotionally and cannot accept that I was once so uncaring, selfish and chaotic. They are finding it hard to put themselves in my life now knowing that I had a record and have been to court so many times. I have never deliberately hidden this part of my life from anyone; especially not friends. It was too hard for me to understand. Let alone knowing how to tell friends in a way that didn't leave me looking like a bad person.

When I say I have changed; I do not say it lightly! I mean I have recreated who I am for the better. Having said that, I don't want anyone to label me fake or un-real. Wouldn't it be so hard to keep up an act for so long? I don't know anyone who would put themselves through so much heartache and pain for the hell of it. I see fire in the eyes of my old soul; and sometimes the old me comes out, but I don't like that person! That is not me! Not anymore.

People see me now as a single mum with 3 children. Working as a consumer advocate, an author and a nice person.

They hear about the times when mental illness took away my ability to parent my children, the ability to function and care about anyone other than myself. They hear about the times that I showed up at court under the influence of drugs (Valium) because I was terrified that if I wasn't medicated I would end up doing something stupid.

The times when I sat on the steps of parliament house begging for someone to help me; and the times when DOCS took my babies away from me. Those times were the lowest and hardest that I have ever gone through!

The picture that is painted when telling my stories to them isn't pretty and I warn them that once they hear it, it can't be Unheard.

Sometimes I feel like I have to apologise for who I used to be ... but then I think FUCK IT!

They didn't know me then and those that were there at that time have had their apologies. I am NOT that person anymore and I refuse to apologise for that part of my life. They were chapters that existed long before they came along. They are parts of ME; not them. I like who I am today. Strong. Independent, conscientious, caring, strong and resilient.

Isn't who I am today worth knowing? Worth getting to know a little more?

I would have thought that given that I am so accepting of others, this only be reciprocated. But sadly society isn't built the same way as me.

Thank you to all those in my life that have heard my stories and accepted them and me; and thankyou to those that walked away because of them. You have made me stronger than I ever dreamed I could be! If ever you should find me alongside you in YOUR life journey; remember that I was worth the effort and you didn't have to walk away.

Fighting in a world where there is no break from reality as it kicks you over and over again, in darkness that only you can see … will either break you or make you.

Remember that I didn't change, the person you became friends with is still here.

Your perception of who you THOUGHT I was or SHOULD be has changed; but not me. Learn the difference and you will see that it was you, not me.

If people are meant to be in your life they will stay no matter what; if they are not supposed to be there then reason will take them away.

Do you know me? Really?

I am a better parent because of mental illness

Yep. I said it. I am a better parent because of mental illness and I will challenge anyone who wants to argue that fact!

Why is it that some people find this statement so shocking?

I believe that my struggles with mental health have made me more aware of my emotions and that in turn has made me have empathy and compassion for my children that I wouldn't necessarily have had. Or to the degree of what I do today; my childhood was tough and the lack of understanding between my parents and myself led to a lot of self- esteem issues, lack of confidence and a feeling of helplessness when life overwhelmed me. Had my parents been more 'in tune' with how I was coping with life; or NOT coping with life, my childhood would be full of good memories rather than bad ones.

When my master 10 isn't travelling well, I can help him get through it. We can talk about it and think of some strategies to help him get control back of the situation.

Using my mental illness as a strength allows me to continue on my recovery journey and I can help my children stay healthy mentally.

I wish that my mother had been more in tune with me and had seen the tears that never fell because I was afraid of letting anyone see that my life was too hard to understand. If she had; we would have not been enemies for so long.

I don't want my children to go through life feeling like I did about my mother and life in general. My boys and I have a great relationship. We can talk to each other about anything and are really close.

Having a mental illness did that and I am so thankful! Bettering me has enabled me to better them for the future, and that's not a bad thing is it?!

I am grateful for the struggles that I have had with my mental illness because I am a more compassionate, empathic and caring parent to my children; and in helping them have good mental wellness, we can ALL help to break down the stigma that the words 'mental illness' bring. If I didn't go through my journey to recovery, I wouldn't be here today to tell the stories that I do.

Having mental health issues DOES NOT make me a bad parent - it makes me a BETTER parent. If you don't agree with this then I CHALLENGE YOU to prove me wrong!

Every day my demons wake ... And every day I fight them and win. As long as I'm the one winning, I take a bet on me!

As well as Borderline Personality Disorder I also suffer from other more physical problems.

I have a chronic illness and chronic pain.

Stage 4 Endometriosis.

Fibromyalgia.

Yay me! Life is a box of fucking chocolates!

NOT.

Over the last 3 years the Endo has slowly taken over major parts of my life. I am very limited in what I can and can't do these days. Mowing the lawns FORGET IT, and that really bothers me because I actually love mowing the lawns. The smell of freshly cut grass on a nice summer's day always made me smile. Hanging clothes on the line is now a thing of the past; the up and down motion of bending and stretching leaves me in agony. Making the beds is no longer something I can do without being in pain for hours after; and running the vacuum over the floors is a job my master 10 now has to do.

He gets paid of course!

I have always suffered from BPD and mental health issues and THAT I could deal with! Hard to understand, but I was able to do a lot more things then that I can't do now.

Having a chronic illness is NOT my choice.

Having a mental illness is NOT my choice.

What IS my choice is what I choose to take from life; and how my experiences and lessons learnt from life, can be taught to others.

I have never said that I have all the answers that you seek; and I don't claim to know how to fix everything that is going on. I can only share what I do that helps me and if someone can get something from that to benefit themselves, then that is enough.

I'm a big girl; I'm overweight, loud, bubbly and friendly. But most people just see me as fat; and although they are correct, they assume that I am lazy and eat constantly. That however is incorrect! I could go to the gym every day and kill myself trying to lose the extra kilos, but once I get home the pain and suffering would be horrendous and my kids will suffer because I am unable to look after them like a mother should.

I would need very strong pain killers, bed rest and a week to recover from the impact that gym session would have on my health. I used to love swimming, but lately even that bring me a lot of pain. A massage used to do the trick and would give me some relief from the pains that my body has; but treating one body ache will aggravate another.

I eat healthy most of the time and love veggies and salad! I am a great cook too, so I spend a lot of time creating healthy food for my family. My weight problems are a result of my health problems; but when people see me they pass judgement – and THAT is what pisses me off the most! Like with anything in life I believe that unless you know the whole story, then you have no business making comment. It is a pity that society isn't the same way.

The people who DO know me have seen through my physical features and seen the real me inside, they love me for who I am and they don't judge me.

I am on the public hospital waiting list for surgery to remove the endometriosis. Who knows how long that will take! Last time I had a similar surgery, instead of it taking 25 minutes it took almost 4 hours. Even knowing this, I still want to put myself through the operation because MAYBE it might help me get control back over my limitations in life.

I am sick of taking 25 tablets a day just so I can make it through. I am still in pain 24/7 but at least I can manage it now.

Yesterday I felt like I was dying. The pain was excruciating and it made me feel sick, I had the sweats and was dizzy and light headed. I was screaming out in agony and nothing I did relieved the torture that was happening inside me. The pain got so bad that I passed out and slept for a while.

I called on a friend to help me, but she wasn't available. So I had to drag myself out of bed to get my boys from school and day-care even though I shouldn't have been driving, I had no choice.

Lying in bed later that afternoon my 10 year old came up to me and asked me if I was going to die; he wanted to call an ambulance because I looked so ill.

It must be bad when your child asks you that huh?

I don't have a strong support network when it comes to needing help with my children, and that causes more stress and anxiety. But as a mother I do what I have to do for them – even if that means risking my health for their sake.

I want my boys to look back when they are older and see that no matter what life sent my way – good or bad, I tackled it head on and did the best that I possibly could. I hope that it is teaching them how to be resilient, strong, and caring people.

No matter what life gives you – make the most of every situation and don't let limitations stop you from being the best you that you can be. Teach your children to be their own hero and remember to tell them that fear is just a word!

Mental illness, chronic pain and illness, plus a salad on the side. They don't belong together! But somehow … it just … works.

If in sharing my experience with others helps to give a voice to those that can no longer speak or find the right words; then I will have saved someone's life and validated my very existence. I should have died but I was saved. I believe THIS is why I am still here on earth. I am to be a teacher to others who are fighting everyday to make it through. I am here to shine a light into the shadows.

I am a survivor of suicide.

I was 'dead' for almost 3 minutes before my heart started beating again.

My life DOES have meaning.

I want to help others to help themselves. I want them to know that we all have a story to tell and we can all learn from each other.

What we go through on a day to day basis when we are in crisis is not only emotional but it is also exhausting!

I want to show people that I was once where they were. I was down and out. I wanted to end my life because I felt worthless and unimportant; but I want them to know that they too can become an important part of the community and they can help others on their own journey. Everyone struggling right now has the ability to change their world and everyone in it.

Lived experience is the best way to learn, educate and understand how we can change the way mental illness is seen by society.

I've shared some of my journey; will you be brave enough to do it too?

I recently came across an envelope that immediately brought fear to my heart. My hands started shaking and my breath started to get faster. It was just a plain pink envelope, nothing special about it other than the words that were etched across the front. 'My babies'. I had not realised that I still had this.

Fear and sadness washed over me; should I open it and read what was inside? Do I want to go back there? Today? Ever? Did finding this envelope mean something? Or does it simply mean that it is time to close that chapter once and for all??

It took me 16 days before I had the courage to decide on what I needed to do.

My hands were trembling when I opened the envelope and took out the single piece of paper that was inside. Tears clouded my vision and it took a few seconds for me to focus on what was written inside.

'You made me life beautiful but I couldn't make life beautiful for you. I'm sorry I couldn't be as strong as you. Never question how much I love you with everything I had inside me. I'm sorry I had to go, but I was just hurting you by staying. Be nothing like me.

Chase your dreams and never let fear stand in your way! Life will be beautiful for you. In my heart I know this. Others will tell you I never loved you enough and that's why I left, but the truth is I love you sooo much that if I stay I think you will end up like me.

Tired, broken and never good enough for anyone! Love each other and love yourself. You are my babies. The only goodness in my world. I don't expect you to forgive me for leaving you. I love you, I love you, I love, I love you!

Never doubt it for a second. I'm sorry I wasn't brave enough to stay.

Love always and forever mum xxxx'

That was it. Less than half a page of writing. That was all I was going to leave behind for my boys. My last words; scrawled on a page and put inside an envelope. No real explanation for why I wasn't going to be there. Had this been all I left behind for my boys, they would have hated me forever!

When you are in THAT moment; when you have made peace with the fact that you will be free from all the pain; you can't think of anything but yourself and how YOU feel.

It all makes sense to you and what I had written in that letter, at the time was enough. For me to write it, and end it - in my head that was all I needed to do.

For a few days after reading this letter I felt so angry and confused. I could not accept that I had been so selfish! Nothing in that letter would bring my babies peace. EVER. They would just see me as a coward who was so selfish that she took the easy way out instead of staying to fight another day.

I've learnt from this whole experience that it shouldn't have to get to this point for a mother to tell her sons that she loves them.

I should not have waited to let them know that I am proud of them and I am a better parent and person simply because they exist in my life. I thank my lucky stars that I am still alive today and that I have been lucky enough to learn from my mistakes.

My boys need me; and they always will. I need them too more than they will ever know. Together we can do anything!

Finding that envelope was a mixture of pain and regret, but it also allowed me to see that live is for living NOW and not to be left to chance. I can tell them I love them whenever I want however many times a day, I can hug them, squeeze them and hold them tight for reasons just because. They will never see this letter, never know that at one point in their lives they almost had to live without their mother.

I know there will be those that judge me for putting this part of my life out in the open, and there will be others that will see me as weak for breaking when it was too much. Regardless of what you may say...I can guarantee you this: If you had made the decision that you were going to die and that it was going to be you that pulled the trigger; you can't think about anyone other than yourself. Because if you could then you were making a really bad decision!

If you or anyone you know are struggling with mental health issues please call lifeline on 13 11 14

For those that rise
beyond the pain and help
create change.